Totally AMAZING FACTS ABOUT REPTILES

ARNOLD RINGSTAD

raintree

a Capstone company — publishers for children

Crocodiles are the **BIGGEST** and **HEAVIEST** reptiles on Earth.

The smallest kind of snake would fit inside the **MOUTH** of the largest kind.

Eek!

4

The dwarf gecko is the smallest reptile. It is about the size of a postage stamp!

5

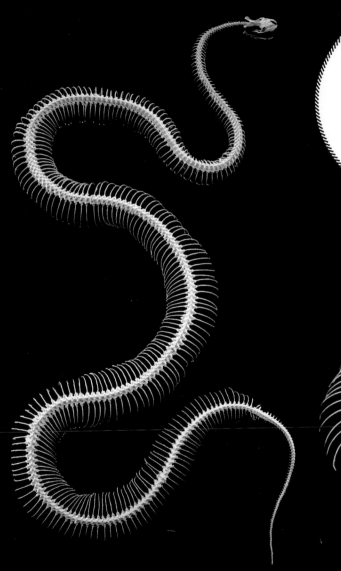
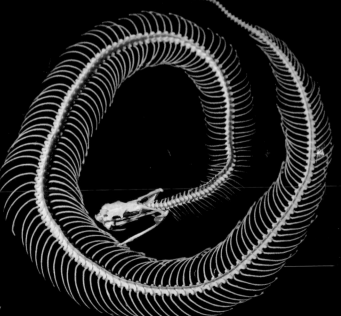

Snakes can have up to 400 vertebrae. Humans have just 33.

6

Some snakes are born with TWO HEADS.

Two heads are better than one!

There are 328 known species of turtles and tortoises.

Tortoises live only on land. Turtles can live on land or in water.

The ancestors of modern snakes had legs. Tiny, useless leg bones can still be seen in some snake species.

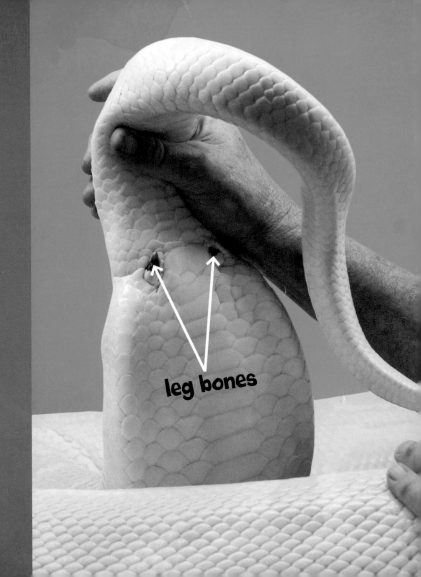

leg bones

There are almost 3,000 known species of snakes.

11

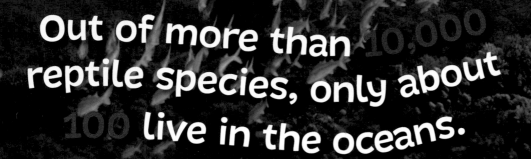

Out of more than 10,000 reptile species, only about 100 live in the oceans.

There are **23** known species of crocodilians.

There are more than **4,600** known species of lizards.

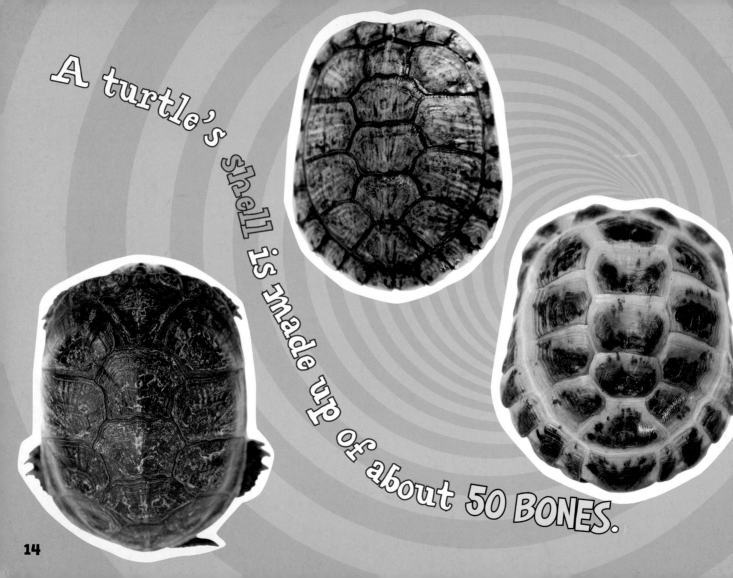

A turtle's shell is made up of about 50 BONES.

A turtle makes room to hide in its shell by blowing air out of its lungs.

15

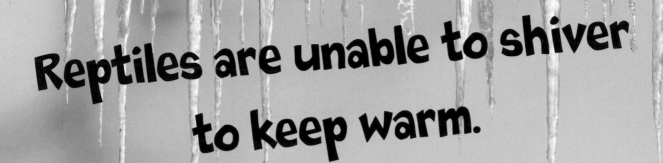

Reptiles are unable to shiver to keep warm.

Brrr! I'm cold!

Some lizards such as the New Guinea tree skink have toxic green blood.

Some kinds of snakes lay just **one** egg. Others lay up to 100!

Male turtles hatch from eggs kept at low temperatures. Female turtles hatch from eggs kept at high temperatures.

19

An adult sea turtle can sleep underwater for six hours without going up for air!

I think I'll just take a short nap . . .

21

There are approximately 270 different types of cobras. They live in warm places such as Asia.

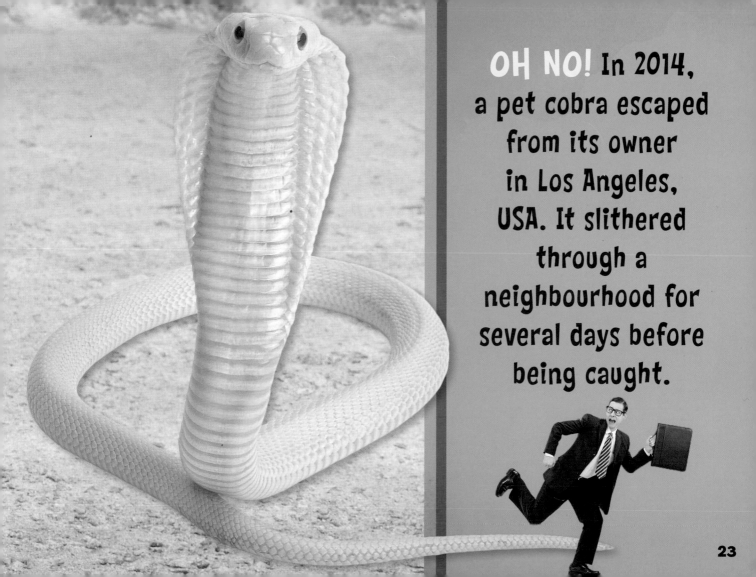

OH NO! In 2014, a pet cobra escaped from its owner in Los Angeles, USA. It slithered through a neighbourhood for several days before being caught.

The eyelash palm pit viper lives in Central America. This snake has scales above each eye that look like EYELASHES.

Don't eat me! I'm not a banana!

The eyelash palm pit viper often hides in banana plants. Many have been accidentally sent all over the world inside banana shipments!

25

The draco
lizard has
wide flaps of
skin. These
flaps allow it
to glide from
tree to tree.

The paradise
flying snake glides
through forests.
It jumps from trees and
flattens its body like
a **PARACHUTE**.

Some lizards can run on their hind legs!

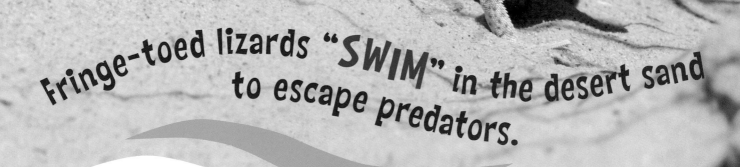

Fringe-toed lizards "SWIM" in the desert sand to escape predators.

Gila monsters store body fat in their tails. They survive on this fat when food is scarce. They can go months without eating.

Gila monsters spend most of their time underground. They mainly eat eggs that they steal from birds' nests.

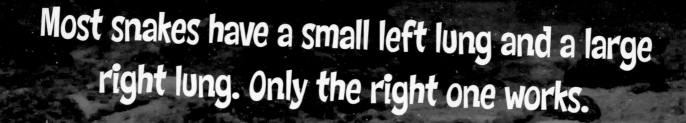

Most snakes have a small left lung and a large right lung. Only the right one works.

Sea snakes like me have only one lung. But we can breathe through our skin!

A snake's fangs are curved backwards. When it takes a bite, its prey finds it hard to escape.

33

Scientists study king cobra venom to make **MEDICINES.**

Is that a pine cone?
No, it's a
shingleback skink!

A shingleback skink's
brown scales make it
look like a
PINE CONE.

The shingleback skink's tail looks like its head. It curls into a C shape to confuse predators.

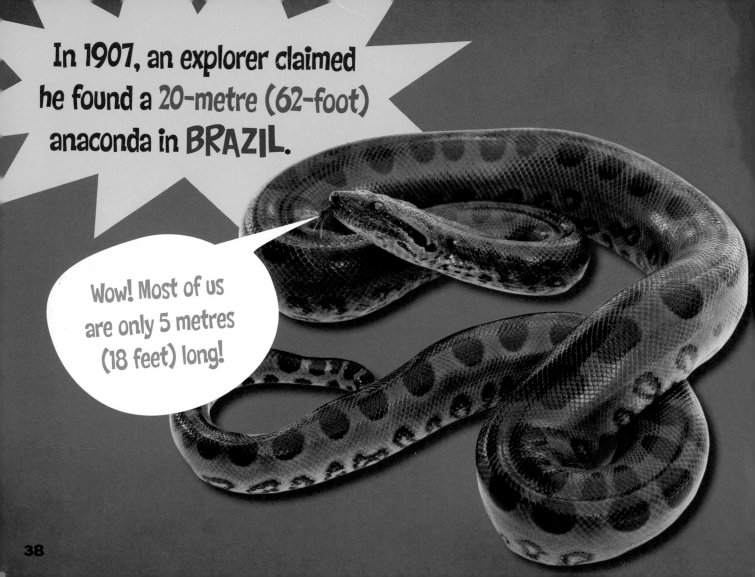

In the 1800s, a scientist heard a rumour that a **MEXICAN** giant musk turtle had chewed its way out of an alligator's stomach!

That's what you get for trying to eat me!

39

Rattlesnakes can **SWIM**. Scientists have found them in the sea several kilometres from shore.

The slender-snouted crocodile in West Africa can climb trees!

TURN UP THE HEAT!

The best temperature for most snakes is about **30 DEGREES CELSIUS** (85 degrees Fahrenheit).

Snakes **SMELL** the world around them about once every second when they're chasing prey.

A snake's forked tongue gives it a 3D view of the smells around it.

Snakes do not have ears. They "hear" by feeling vibrations in the ground.

A group of turtles is called a **BALE**.

A group of anacondas is called a **KNOT**.

A group of crocodiles is called a **BASK**.

When snakes bite into prey, they can lose teeth! But they constantly grow **NEW** ones.

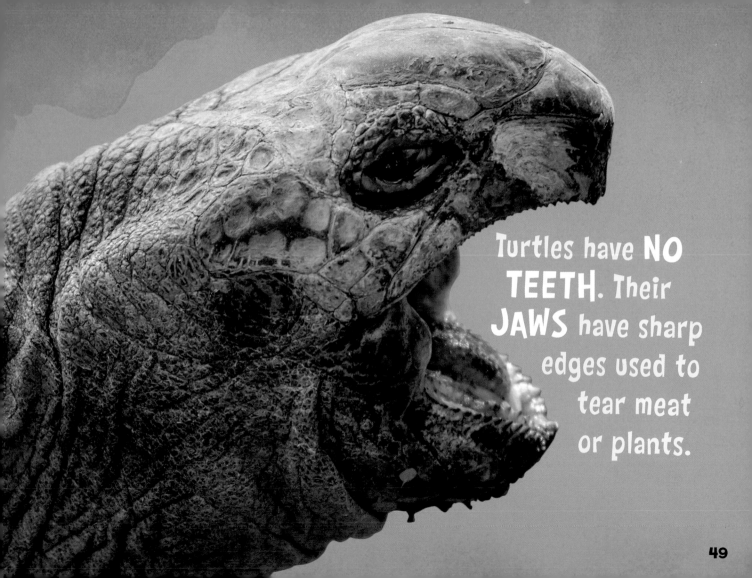

Turtles have **NO TEETH**. Their **JAWS** have sharp edges used to tear meat or plants.

The **armadillo lizard**
curls into a ball
and puts its
tail into its
mouth to
protect
itself.

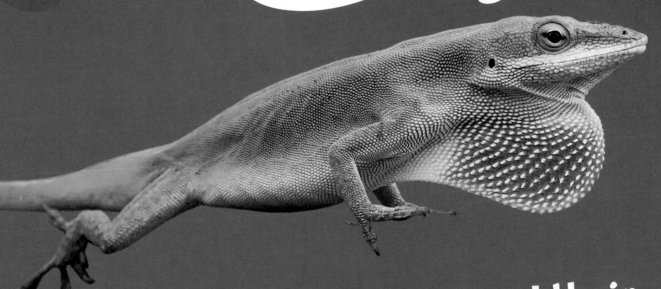

Male anole lizards expand their throats when they see a snake.

51

Alligators grow new teeth as old ones wear out.

One alligator may go through as many as **3,000 TEETH** in a lifetime!

Markings on the Indian cobra look like **LARGE EYES**.

The "eyes" trick predators into thinking the snake is larger than it really is.

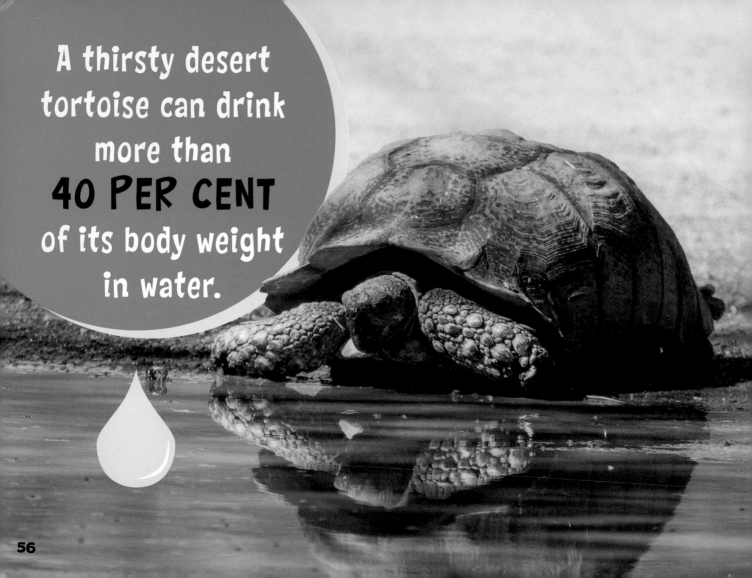

A thirsty desert tortoise can drink more than **40 PER CENT** of its body weight in water.

For a 45-kilogram (100-pound) person, that's like drinking **18.9 LITRES (5 GALLONS)** of water!

A mother Nile crocodile rolls her eggs in her mouth. The movement helps the baby crocs hatch from the eggs.

Some crocodile mothers let their babies swim into their **MOUTHS** for protection.

A Komodo dragon can eat up to **80 PER CENT** of its body weight in just one meal.

A Komodo dragon can eat 2.5 kilograms (5.5 pounds) of meat in just one minute. That's like eating more than **20 HAMBURGERS!**

61

Box turtles often spend their entire lives in an area about the size of a **FOOTBALL PITCH**.

In Arizona, USA, the desert box turtle sometimes beats the heat by burrowing into fresh **COW POO**.

63

Some tortoises can live to be more than 150 years old.

The Labord's chameleon lives for just four or five months.

It spends more time in its egg than out of it!

65

A Burmese python UNHINGES its jaw to swallow huge prey.

The African rock python suffocates its prey and swallows it **WHOLE**.

This snake can eat antelopes and crocodiles!

Young green
sea turtles are
OMNIVORES - they eat
both meat and plants.

But when they reach
22 kilograms (10 pounds)
in weight, they become
HERBIVORES.
They eat only plants.

Vipers can fold away their **FANGS** until needed.

The Gaboon viper has the **LONGEST** fangs of any snake.

Its fangs grow up to **5 CENTIMETRES** (2 inches) long!

A chameleon can move its two eyes **SEPARATELY**. It can see two different objects at the same time.

Some chameleons can shoot out their **TONGUES** as far as the length of their bodies!

73

Geckos have **HOOKS** on their feet that allow them to walk on walls or even ceilings.

The Berlandier's tortoise eats the **DROPPINGS** of other tortoises.

Yum!

76

Leatherback sea turtles can eat dozens of JELLYFISH in a single meal.

Time for a snack!

The coast horned lizard of California, USA, sprays predators with **BLOOD** from its eyes.

The musk turtle is known as the **STINKPOT** turtle.

It gives off terrible odours to scare off predators.

79

Snakes can detect temperature changes of just **0.001°C (0.002°F).**

This ability helps them find prey in darkness.

Pit vipers sense body heat using an organ between their eyes.

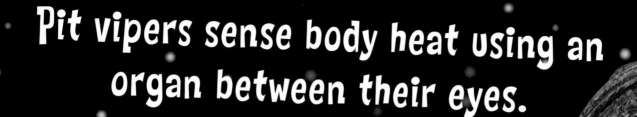

Scientists blindfolded a pit viper, and it was still able to catch its prey.

The earliest known turtles lived 220 million years ago.

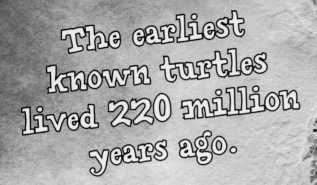

Wow! I have some pretty cool ancestors!

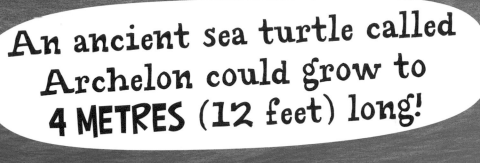

An ancient sea turtle called Archelon could grow to **4 METRES** (12 feet) long!

Adult Komodo dragons sometimes **EAT BABY** Komodo dragons.

Baby Komodo dragons roll around in the **GUTS OF DEAD** animals to hide their scent from hungry adult Komodo dragons.

Scientists call the tuatara a **"LIVING FOSSIL"** because it's related to reptiles that lived during the time of the dinosaurs.

A tuatara has a third eye that's used to **SENSE LIGHT**. The eye helps the tuatara tell what time it is!

Thorny devil lizards inflate their chests to look **BIGGER**.

They have **SPIKES** on their bodies that make it difficult for predators to swallow them.

Geckos are NOISY!

They chirp, click, squeak and growl.

The Cuban crocodile hunts **BIRDS**.

It uses its tail to launch itself into the air from underwater.

92

The green
tree python
hunts by
DANGLING
its tail as
bait from a
tree branch.

Puff adders and cobras **INFLATE** the front of their bodies to appear larger when threatened.

A frilled lizard opens its neck flaps like an **UMBRELLA** to scare away predators.

Geckos **SHED THEIR TAILS** when threatened. The tail distracts the predator so the lizard can escape.

Lizards that lose their tails can **GROW THEM BACK.**

Crocodiles bite with a force of up to **350 KILOGRAMS** per square centimetre (5,000 pounds per square inch).

98

Human **BITES** are a wimpy
**7 KILOGRAMS PER
SQUARE CENTIMETRE**
(100 pounds per square inch).

99

Anacondas can eat large animals such as deer and small crocodiles.

After a big meal, they can go weeks **WITHOUT EATING** again.

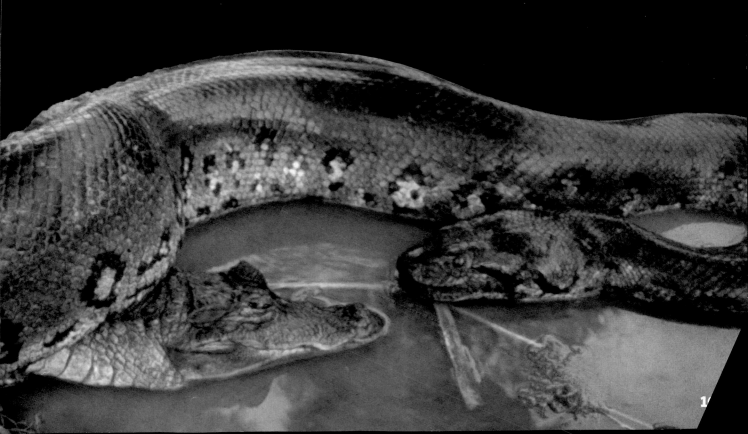

The alligator snapping turtle has a wormlike "LURE" on the tip of its tongue. The turtle uses it to catch fish!

The North American wood turtle stomps its feet to bring **EARTHWORMS** to the surface. Then it eats them!

The green basilisk lizard has long, wide toes that allow it to dash across water for about **4.5 METRES** (15 feet).

Desert sidewinder snakes throw their bodies in **LOOPS** across the sand to zoom along hot dunes.

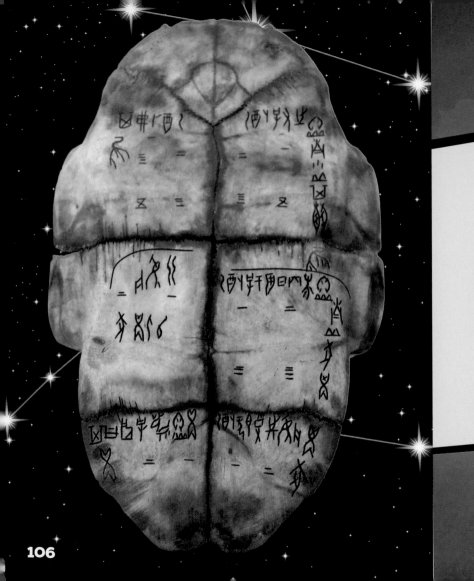

In ancient China, the patterns on tortoise shells were believed to predict the **FUTURE**.

The Soviet Union, now Russia, launched two tortoises into space in 1968.

Australia's deserts have the most lizard varieties. In some places, up to **40 SPECIES** live in the same area.

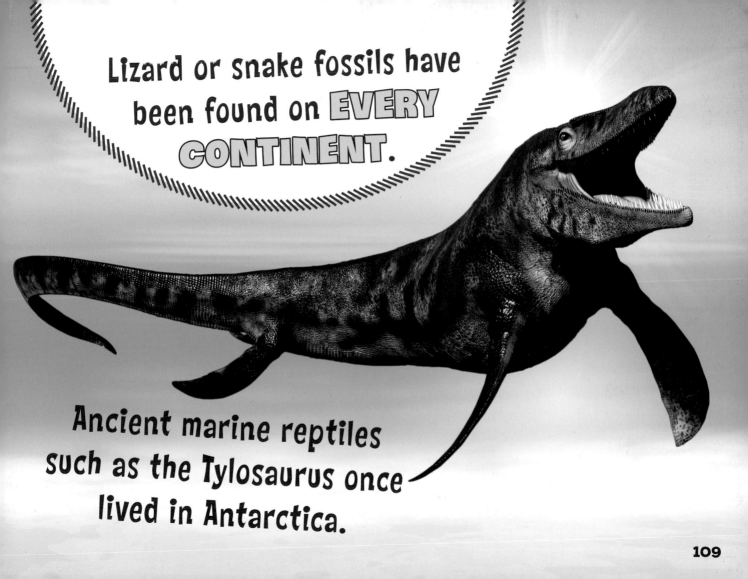

Lizard or snake fossils have been found on EVERY CONTINENT.

Ancient marine reptiles such as the Tylosaurus once lived in Antarctica.

GLOSSARY

ancestors prehistoric animals that are related to modern animals

burrow dig a hole or a tunnel

fangs long pointed teeth

fossil remains or traces of an animal that lived millions of years ago

herbivore animal that eats only plants

inflate fill up with air or gas

marine living in the sea

omnivore animal that eats both plants and meat

predators animal or insect that hunts other animals for food

prey animal that is hunted by another animal for food

species group of animals that have similar features

suffocate kill something by cutting off its air supply

venom poisonous liquid used by some snakes when they bite

vertebrae small bones that form an animal's spine

FIND OUT MORE

BOOKS

Reptiles (Explorers), Claire Llewellyn (Kingfisher, 2013)

Snakes and Lizards (Really Weird Animals), Clare Hibbert (Franklin Watts, 2015)

WEBSITES

www.bbc.co.uk/guides/zp9pfg8
Find out more about reptiles on this website.

www.ngkids.co.uk/animals/turtle-facts
Read 10 fun facts about turtles!

INDEX

Raintree is an imprint of Capstone Global Library Limited, a company incorporated in England and Wales having its registered office at 264 Banbury Road, Oxford, OX2 7DY – Registered company number: 6695582

www.raintree.co.uk
myorders@raintree.co.uk

Text © Capstone Global Library Limited 2018

Edited by Maddie Spalding
Designed by Kazuko Collins
Original illustrations © Capstone Global Library Ltd 2018
Picture research by Maddie Spalding
Production by Laura Polzin and Kazuko Collins
Printed and bound in China.

ISBN 978 1 4747 4289 4
21 20 19 18 17
10 9 8 7 6 5 4 3 2 1

British Library Cataloguing in Publication Data
A full catalogue record for this book is available from the British Library.

Acknowledgements
We would like to thank the following for permission to reproduce photographs:
Alamy: Anna Yu, 36–37, Danita Delimont, 104, Gina Kelly, 10, Hira Punjabi, 28, Marion Kaplan, 41, MisFitt, 21, Rick & Nora Bowers, 31, Sgt. Brian Calhoun/PJF Military Collection, 40; iStockphoto: AlinaMD, 22–23, CathyKeifer, 73, Colonel 78 (blood), Dendenal81, 3, draskovic, 6 (left), drferry, 25 (snake), GlobalP, 15, kellyvandellen, 49, lilu330, 72 (eyes), liveslow, 11 (left snake), Meilun, 107 (helmets), neyro2008, 74–75 (gecko footprints), Niteenrk, 25 (bananas), Photo2008, 62 (turtle), photosbyjimn, 13 (bottom), PomInOz, 2, reptiles4all, 44 (left snake), 50, rez-art/Thinkstock, 61 (background), saiko3p, 47, Serge_Vero, 9, sirichaicr, 5 (stamp), USO, 98, yuoak, 76 (plate); Newscom: Cede Prudente/NHPA/Photoshot, 27; Science Source: Anthony Bannister, 34–35, Chris Mattison, 65, Frans Lanting/MINT Images, 26, James L. Amos, 87, John Mitchell, 66, M. Watson, 46 (anacondas), 58, Martin Harvey, 59, Michael McCoy, 17, Michael Patrick O'Neill, 77 (sea turtle), Peter Chadwick, 67, Yoshiharu Sekino, 100–101; Shutterstock: Agustin Esmoris, 76 (droppings), Andrei Mayatnik, 46 (turtles), Andrej Sevkovskij, 54, ANGHI, 36 (pinecone), Anna Kucherova, cover (top right), benchart, 107 (spaceship), BERNATSKAYA OXANA, 103 (bottom), bluedog studio, 18, Brook Harris, 43 (snake), Butterfly Hunter, 48, Caron Badkin, 90, Cathy Keifer, 72, chamleunejai, 4 (large snake), Chris Watson, 88, Chuck Rausin, 33 (top snake), cynoclub, 107 (tortoises), Dr Morley Read, 74, Eky Studio, cover, 10, 13, 23, 26, 28, 33, 36, 38–39, 44, 48, 49, 50, 51, 53, 63, 64–65, 67, 68, 73, 106, 110, 111, 112, Eric Isselee, 7, espies, 61 (foreground), Evgenya Brooth, 28 (smoke), FatJackey, 108, fivespots, cover (bottom right), 11 (right snake), 39 (turtle), 79, 103 (top), Gudkov Andrey, 60, H.Tanaka, 77 (jellyfish), Issarawat Tattong, 57, Jason Mintzer, 29, jeep2499, 6 (right), Jenny Sturm, 64, kaman985shu, 52–53, Kenishirotie, 99, KentaStudio, 94, Kjersti Joergensen, 84, kkaplin, cover (top left), Kristian Bell, 42 (snake), Leena Robinson, 51 (lizard), Ljupco Smokovski, 23 (business man), lokvi, 63 (turtle), Longjourneys, 20, Lucian Coman, cover (bottom left), lunatic67, 93, Marcus England, 78, Matt Cornish, 95, Matt Jeppson, 45, 96–97, Matteo photos, 70–71, Michael Rosskothen, 83, Mr Twister, 16 (icicles), Muangsatun, 63 (poop), MZPHOTO.CZ, 91 (bottom), Papa Bravo, 75, Patrick K. Campbell, 38, PorKaliver, 33 (bottom snake), Pranesh Luckan, 56, reptiles4all, 5, 23 (pink snake), 24, 39 (alligator), 70, 81, 91 (top), 102, back cover, Rich Carey, 32, Roger de Montfort, 105, Rosa Jay, 14, Ross Gordon Henry, 86, schwarzhana, 92 (right), seasoning_17, 19, Sergei Prokhorov, 106, Sergey Uryadnikov, 85, 92 (left), SOMKKU, 62 (background), somyot pattana, 4 (small snake), Sonsedska Yuliia, 80, spatuletail, 82 (fossil), Starover Sibiriak, 16, stephan kerkhofs, 68–69, stockakia, 42 (thermometer), 43 (thermometer), Studio DMM Photography, Designs & Art, 82 (turtle), Tallllly, 44 (right snake), Thorsten Rust, 13 (top), Uwe Bergwitz, 89, Vladimir Wrangel, 8, 76 (tortoise), Volodymyr Krasyuk, 43 (ice), Warpaint, 109, Willyam Bradberry, 12

Design Elements: Red Line Editorial, Shutterstock Images and iStockphoto

Every effort has been made to contact copyright holders of material reproduced in this book. Any omissions will be rectified in subsequent printings if notice is given to the publisher.

All the internet addresses (URLs) given in this book were valid at the time of going to press. However, due to the dynamic nature of the internet, some addresses may have changed, or sites may have changed or ceased to exist since publication. While the author and publisher regret any inconvenience this may cause readers, no responsibility for any such changes can be accepted by either the author or the publisher.